Who Lives Here?

An introduction to tracking and identification skills in the temperate mixed and broadleaf forests of North America

For Dot and Gwen

Written and illustrated by:

Cee Thorketil

Welcome to the temperate broadleaf and mixed forest of North America!

Among the oaks,

maples,

and pines,

you can discover many animal signs!

Finding tracks is super fun!

Look!

You just found your first one!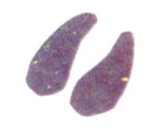

Who could it be?

Follow the tracks

and you will see!

Track Facts

TOES: 2

SIZE: medium

SPECIAL CLUE: toes can spread

Who naps in the grass so long,
while the robin in the oak tree sings a song?
It's a white-tailed fawn!

Look!

A SECOND animal track!

Who could it be?

Follow the tracks

and you will see!

Track Facts

TOES: 4

SIZE: medium-large

SPECIAL CLUE: X shape between toes and heel

It's a COYOTE with her cute little CUBS! These SONG DOGS have a lot to say!

Yippy-
Yippity- yap!
AROOO!

It means, "Hello family! How are you?"
Did you see the lady slippers in bloom today?

Look!

Another track!

Who could it be?

Follow the tracks

and you will see!

Track Facts

TOES: 5
SIZE: small
SPECIAL CLUE: found near water

Look!

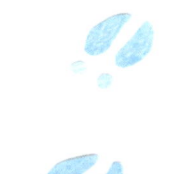

A fourth track!

WHO could it be?

Follow the tracks

and you will see!

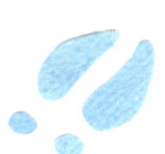

TRACK FACTS

TOES: 2 toes, 2 dew claws

SIZE: extra large

SPECIAL CLUE: MASSIVE!

Look!

Another track!

WHO could it be?

Follow the tracks

and you will see!

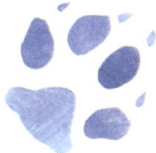

Track Facts

TOES: 4

SIZE: medium

SPECIAL CLUE: diamond shape

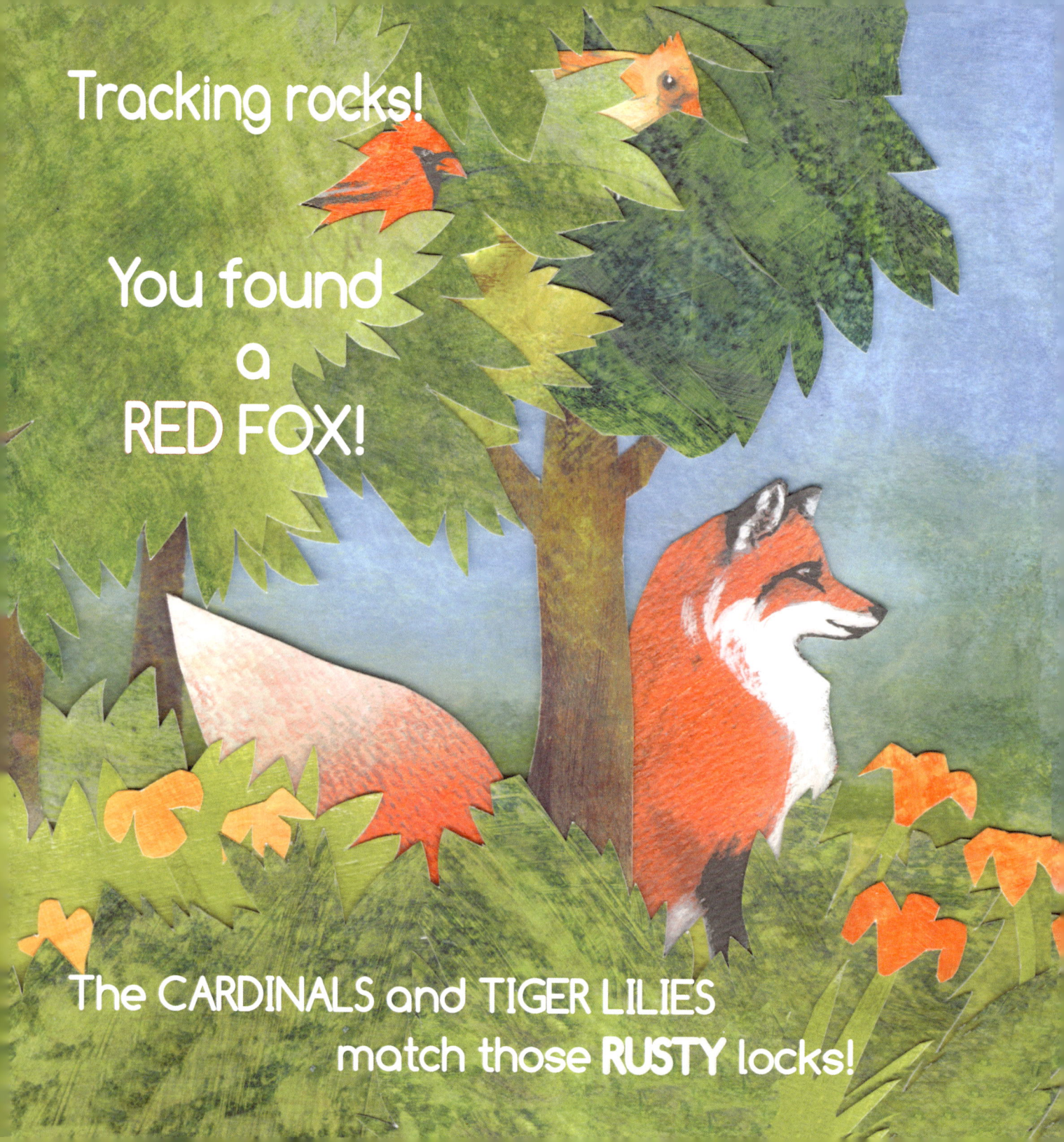

Look!

A sixth track!

Who could it be?

Follow the tracks

and you will see!

Track Facts

TOES: 5

SIZE: small-medium

SPECIAL CLUE: opposable thumbs

Who else has opposable thumbs? It's the opossum!

Much like a koala bear, they have a pouch but with room to spare!

Look!

A seventh track?!

WHO could it be?

Follow the tracks

and you will see!

Track Facts

TOES: 0

SIZE: small

SPECIAL CLUE: wavy line

It's a garter snake sunbathing on the rock. Snakes have no feet, of course, they cannot walk.

The golden chanterelle mushroom and wintergreen berries look so good, they can even be **foraged** for human food!

Look!

An eighth track!

Who could it be?

Follow the tracks

and you will see!

Track Facts
TOES: 5
SIZE: small- medium
SPECIAL CLUE: long heart shaped heel pad

Look!

A ninth set of prints!

WHO could it be?

Follow the tracks

and you will see!

Track Facts

TOES: 3

SIZE: large

SPECIAL CLUE: triangular shape

Look!

A tenth track!

Who could it be?

Follow the tracks

and you will see!

Track Facts

TOES: 4 front, 5 hind

SIZE: medium

SPECIAL CLUE: palm creases often visible

It's a PORCUPINE!

Porcupines like to dine on hemlock trees in the winter time.

Hello, cardinals in the trees, and blue jay flying in the breeze!

Look!

An eleventh track!

Who could it be?

Follow the tracks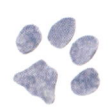

and you will see!

Track Facts
TOES: 4
SIZE: medium-large
SPECIAL CLUE: no claw marks

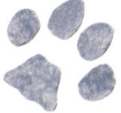

A beautiful sight!

 A bobcat and her bobkitten take a nap in the moonlight.

Bobkittens stay with their mom to learn skills, like how to hunt and avoid porcupine quills.

The more you learn about nature

the more FUN it is to EXPLORE!

You've just met eleven

creatures and there are so

many MORE!

Living in harmony

among the trees,

they make the forest

a special place to be!

Animal Tracks
Look for tracks in snow, sand, or soil

White-tailed deer

Coyote, AKA Song Dog

American Mink

Moose

Red Fox

Opossum

Garter Snake

Striped Skunk

Wild Turkey

Porcupine

Bobcat

    I began creating this book for my daughter, Gwen, but soon realized I wanted to share it with others who feel inspired by the nature around us.

    My hope is that every child can build a connection with nature— not only for the healing, peace, and beauty it brings to the heart, but also to inspire care and protection for the wild beings I care so deeply about.

~*Cee*

Use this QR code, or go to www.bardowlarts.com/bonusprints to print your free guide!

If the art featured in this book captures your heart, swing by my Etsy shop, Bard Owl Arts! You'll find stunning archival-quality prints, both framed and unframed, enchanted forest and fantasy-themed play mats inspired by role playing games like D&D, plus adorable apparel for young nature lovers!

Copyright © 2025 by Christine Grimes AKA Cee Thorketil and Bard Owl Farm LLC

No portion of this book may be reproduced in any form without

written permission from the publisher or author, except as permitted by U.S. copyright law.

All rights reserved. www.bardowlarts.com

May all beings be happy and free from suffering— love to all, great and small.

www.ingramcontent.com/pod-product-compliance
Lightning Source LLC
LaVergne TN
LVRC091353060526
838201LV00019B/290